Acknowledgements

This project would never have happened without the ... ...mo, like me, is a wild-eyed enthusiast, though he has vastly more convincing and committed facial h... ...n Gilbert, Managing Director of Independent Thinking Limited, who allowed it. The drive behind the project, though, came from Jo Robson and Susan Biggs of *Playing for Success*. These two ladies have been instrumental in turning the 'What if?' into the 'How?'

Thanks are due to Crystal Palace FC, particularly the Deputy Chairman, Dominic Holland, and to both John Murphy and Glen Denham, respectively Executive Principal and Principal of *Oasis Academy: Shirley Park* who saw worth in the project at an early stage. Thanks too to the boys involved: Antonio Cardazzone being particularly influential in getting the other boys on board.

Thanks also to Caroline Lenton of Crown House and Tom Fitton; to Geraldine Cooke of the Marsh Agency, my literary agent, for advising me on a venture that was always going to make substantially less than zero profit. Finally, thanks are due to the enormously talented illustrator, Paul Bryant, of The Times of London, who has worked skillfully, without complaining at the absurd deadlines he has been given, and produced, I think, something to be proud of. He is a class act, and truly class acts are rare indeed.

First published by Inspired Education Books www.inspired-education.co.uk

10-digit ISBN 184590420-6
13-digit ISBN 978-184590420-3

Printed and bound in the UK by
The Gomer Press, Llandysul

Activity One – stretching exercises

Objective
To introduce the shapes of punctuation marks and embed these through muscle memory.

Grouping
Whole class (16 kids) seated in a circle.

Activity
1. Players to lie on their backs in a circle, knees raised.
2. Keeping the left foot on the floor, left knee bent, players use their right foot to trace out the shapes of the punctuation marks in the following order: full stop, comma, question mark, exclamation mark, apostrophe, colon, semi colon, ellipsis, dash, hyphen
3. Back to starting positions.
4. Keeping their feet together, players raise both diagonally and to the left, straight legged, indicating the first set of speech marks with their feet. They immediately swing these to the right and indicate the closing speech marks.
5. Legs are then parted in a 'V' shape, and inverted commas are indicated.
6. Back to starting positions.
7. Repeat step two with the right foot.

Activity Two – warm up

Objective

To introduce punctuation as signalling intervals of time for the reader.

Grouping

Whole class (16 kids) standing at corner flag.

Activity

1. Players jog around the perimeter of the pitch as a group.
2. Coach shouts out one of the following: comma, semi colon, colon, period, ellipsis. Players immediately follow the command, making the appropriate action and sound, then return to jogging.
3. On the shout of "comma" players bend down and touch the pitch in the following manner, making the sound "shhhh."
4. On the shout of "semi colon" players bend down and touch the pitch twice: hitting it once to the sound of "huh," then immediately follow this with the comma action and sound.
5. On the shout of "colon" players bend down and hit the pitch twice to the sound of "huh," then count a further one before they return to jogging.
6. On the shout of "period: players hit the pitch once to the sound of "huh," but stay knelt down for a further count of three before they return to jogging.
7. On the shout of "ellipsis" players bend down and hit the floor three times, going from left to right to the sound of "huh, huh, huh."

Activity Three – Warm up 2 - Use of the comma 1

Objective

To teach a range of connectives

To establish that these are generally prefixed by a comma

To teach that there are two forms of connective: those showing a positive causal effect driving a sentence forward (connectives – and, then, so), and those that show negative causal effect, making the sentence reverse on itself (counter connectives – however, but, although).

Grouping

Whole class standing in a circle with coach. One football required.

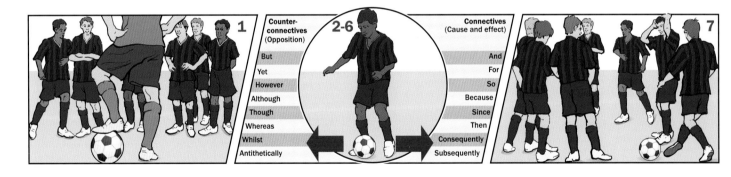

Activity

1. Coach to start with ball at his feet, explain that a connective joins two phrases together that would otherwise be discreet sentences. Example: "Steve is a good player. He needs to concentrate on his passing." is two sentences. To make a compound sentence, you join them together with a connective. Either a 'straight connective' which joins the two phrases in a forward momentum "Steve is a good

player, and he needs to concentrate on his passing." Or a 'counter connective' which shows a negative causal effect, "Steve is a good player, but he needs to concentrate on his passing." Coach to explain that connectives are generally prefixed by a comma.

2. Coach then says either 'connective' or 'counter connective', and then passes the ball to one of the players next to him in the circle. If he says 'connective' he will pass the ball to the left. If he says 'counter connective' he passes the ball to the right.

3. The receiving player then makes the decision to say either 'connective' or counter connective'. If he chooses 'connective' he passes the ball to the next player the way the ball was going: ie. if he has received the ball from the left, he will pass the ball in the same direction it was going – to the player directly to the right of him. If, however, he decides on 'counter connective' he will pass the ball back to the person who has passed it to him; if he has received it from the right, he will pass it back to his left.

4. Trial this a few times. Until players are fluent in it. When it breaks down, or a player makes a mistake, the ball goes back to the coach.

5. The coach then expands the vocabulary of the session to include 'and' as a connective, and 'but' as a counter connective. Players continue the game saying 'and' or 'connective' to pass the ball the way it was going, and 'but' or 'counter connective' to reverse the path of the ball.

6. Practice this until it is embedded, then gradually expand the vocabulary with the following table:

Connectives (Cause + Effect)	Counter-connectives (Opposition)
And	But
For	Yet
So	However
Because	Although
Since	Though
Then	Whereas
Consequently	Whilst
Subsequently	Antithetically

7. When all connectives are in operation, play the game seriously. When someone makes a mistake they have to come out of the circle. Play until such point as there are only two players and the coach left. The last player to make a mistake at this point is the winner.

Activity Four – More on connectives

Objective

To embed knowledge of the variety of connectives

To embed that these generally have a comma before them

Grouping

Players stand individually, equally spaced, along the half way line, ball at their feet.

Activity

1. Players are asked to dribble the ball slowly towards the goal line.

2. Coach teaches the Cruyff drag back

3. Coach shouts out a variety of the connectives already used. Where the coach shouts out a straight 'connective' players must place their foot on the ball and then drag the ball back, in the shape of a comma, then continue dribbling the way they are facing. Where the coach shouts out a 'counter connective', they perform a Cruyff drag back, reversing their direction and then continue dribbling in the new direction.

Activity Five – Use of the comma 2

Objective

To establish that commas are used before opening direct speech.

Grouping

Players stand in two queues of eight behind the half way line.

Activity

1. Coach explains the rules of laying out direct speech. It is marked off with a comma, then opening speech marks, then a capital letter, the text, a full stop; and finally closing speech marks. Explain that the speech marks go outside of the other punctuation.

2. Coach exemplifies the moves: a half drag back with the right foot for a comma; tapping the ball twice with the left foot for the opening speech marks; scooping the ball up with either foot for the capital letter; a brief dribble for the text; foot on the ball for the full stop; tap the ball twice with the right foot for the closing speech marks.

3. Players follow this sequence, shouting out the names of the punctuation marks as they perform the requisite moves in the requisite order. "Comma," (drag back with the right foot), "Open speech marks," (tap ball twice with left foot), "Capital," (scoop the ball up with either foot), "Text," (brief, mazy dribble), "Full stop," (foot on the ball), "Close speech marks," (tap the ball twice with the right foot), "Goal," (shoot).

Activity Seven – Use of the comma 4 - Gladiators

Objective

To establish that commas are used immediately after the adverb in a sentence with an adverbial start.

Grouping

Two squares are marked out with cones. Eight players in each square. Each player has a ball.

Activity

1. The object of the game is simple, you dribble within the square attempting to keep whole of your own ball, whilst also attempting to kick other players' balls out of the square. When your ball is kicked out of the square, you are out. The last player whose ball is in the square is the winner.

2. However, when the coach shouts out an adjective, the players must immediately shout the word, "Comma," back at the coach, and, whatever they are doing, place their foot on the ball, dragging it back to signify the coma. They must then continue playing the game in the manner of the adverb. For instance, if the coach shouts the adverb, "Bravely," they must place their foot on the ball, dragging it back to signify the coma, and then continue playing in a brave manner.

List of Adverbs		
boldly	gracefully	safely
bravely	hastily	sharply
calmly	lazily	slowly
carefully	neatly	smoothly
carelessly	perfectly	softly
cautiously	powerfully	speedily
cleverly	quickly	suddenly
deliberately	rapidly	swiftly
elegantly	recklessly	thoughtfully
enthusiastically	regularly	tightly
gently	roughly	wildly

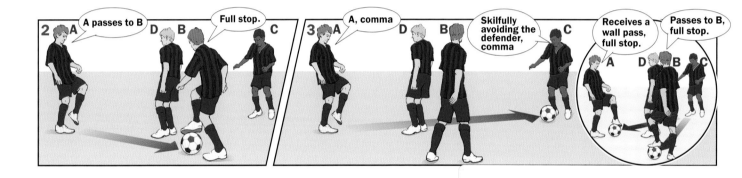